Beatrix Potter

My Favorite Writer

Jennifer Hurtig

WEIGL PUBLISHERS INC.

Published by Weigl Publishers Inc.
350 5th Avenue, Suite 3304, PMB 6G
New York, NY 10118-0069

Website: www.weigl.com

Library of Congress Cataloging-in-Publication Data

Hurtig, Jennifer.
  Beatrix Potter : my favorite writer / Jennifer Hurtig.
     p. cm.
  Includes index.
  ISBN 978-1-59036-922-7 (hard cover : alk. paper) -- ISBN 978-1-
59036-923-4 (soft cover : alk. paper)
  1. Potter, Beatrix, 1866-1943--Juvenile literature. 2. Authors, English--
20th century--Biography--Juvenile literature. 3. Artists--Great Britain--
Biography--Juvenile literature. 4. Children's stories--Authorship--Juvenile
literature. I. Title.
  PR6031.O72Z5876 2009
  823'.912--dc22
  [B]   2008003968

Printed in the United States of America
1 2 3 4 5 6 7 8 9 0 12 11 10 09 08

Project Coordinator
Heather C. Hudak

Design
Terry Paulhus

Contents

Beatrix Potter

MILESTONES

1866 Born on July 28, in Bolton Gardens, South Kensington, London

1881 Develops a secret code, which she uses to write journal entries

1885 Brings home her first pet rabbit, which she names Benjamin Bouncer

1890 Sells drawings of her rabbit to Hildesheimer & Faulkner to be used in cards and a book of rhymes

1895 A series of drawings titled *A Frog he would a-fishing go* are purchased for use in a children's book

1901 Privately publishes *The Tale of Peter Rabbit*

1905 Becomes engaged to Norman Warne, who dies soon after

1905 Buys Hill Top, a farm in Sawrey, Lancashire

1913 Marries William Heelis

1921 The first French edition of *The Tale of Peter Rabbit* is published

1943 Elected the first female president of the Herdwick Sheepbreeders' Association

1943 Dies on December 22, in Sawrey, Lancashire

Beatrix Potter created some of the best-beloved books of all time, including *The Tale of Peter Rabbit*. Beatrix's books take young readers on a wonderful journey into the make-believe world of mischief-making, talking animals.

As a child, Beatrix did not have many friends, so she spent most of her time reading, studying, drawing, and writing. She wrote stories and drew pictures of her pets, as well as animals she saw on farms and in the countryside.

Over time, Beatrix's friends and family encouraged her to share her stories with the world. She looked for ways to publish her work, finding success in the early 1900s. For years, Beatrix wrote and illustrated many tales about whimsical animals. Children all over the world enjoyed reading her books, and young readers continue to cherish these stories.

Today, Beatrix Potter's original drawings are kept in museums and galleries. Movies, a ballet, and stage shows have been made about her life. Exhibitions around the world and timeless stories have brought her work to people everywhere.

Early Childhood

Helen Beatrix Potter was born on July 28, 1866, in London, England. Her father was a wealthy lawyer. Beatrix's parents were busy with work and other activities, so Beatrix was raised mainly by servants and **governesses**. She was taught at home, where the governesses encouraged her to write and draw.

When Beatrix was six years old, her brother Bertram was born. Bertram went away to boarding school when he was 11 and Beatrix was 17. Each year, the family took long summer holidays in Scotland and, later, the English **Lake District**.

When on vacation, Beatrix and Bertram would play in the woods. There, they saw many animals. They even tamed some of the animals they found.

London is the capital of England and Great Britain.

At home, Beatrix had many pets, including mice, rabbits, frogs, bats, and a hedgehog. Benjamin Bouncer was Beatrix's first pet rabbit. She purchased him from a bird shop in London and brought him home without her parents knowing. Peter Piper was another of Beatrix's rabbits. He was a Belgian buck rabbit and could learn tricks, such as jumping through a hoop, or ringing a bell. Mrs. Tiggy-winkle was Beatrix's pet hedgehog. She often traveled with Beatrix on the train, and she was always hungry. Spot the spaniel was the family's dog. Spot liked to travel in **carriages**. Later in life, Beatrix made pets of some of her farm animals. Pig-Wig was a black Berkshire pig that she bought from a pig farmer. She bottle-fed the pig and kept it in a basket beside her bed. She also had many farm dogs.

Beatrix studied the way her animals lived. She knew a great deal about how they would behave and the types of activities they enjoyed. Beatrix later used this information to write lively stories and draw detailed pictures.

Beatrix began to make drawings of her pets and the animals she saw when she was on summer vacation.

Growing Up

Beatrix began writing in a journal when she was 15 years of age. She wrote in a secret code using very tiny print. Only Beatrix knew how to read the text. She continued writing in this way until she was 31. No one knows why Beatrix chose to write in code, and the code was not broken until many years after her death.

In 1893, Beatrix began writing tales of her animal friends in letters to Noel Moore. Noel was the child of one of Beatrix's former governesses. Noel became ill when he was five years old. Beatrix made up stories and drawings to entertain him. In one letter, she wrote the story of Peter Rabbit, along with pictures.

"I remember I used to half believe and wholly play with fairies when I was a child."
Beatrix Potter

Beatrix's letters to Noel became the basis for many of her books.

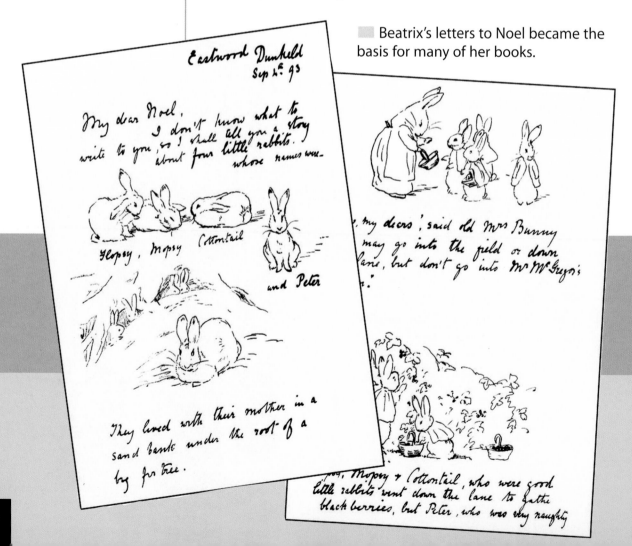

By this time, Beatrix was earning some money by writing and drawing greeting cards and book illustrations. In 1890, she earned a small fee for illustrations that she sent to the German card company Hildesheimer & Faulkner. The company asked Beatrix to send more. Three years later, Hildesheimer & Faulkner **commissioned** Beatrix to illustrate a book of children's verses, called *The Happy Pair*, by Frederic E. Weatherly.

During the 1890s, Beatrix was very interested in plants. She lived near the Natural History Museum and often went to the museum to learn about different kinds of **fungi**. She also spent many hours drawing fungi and painting them in watercolor. Beatrix even wrote **theories** about lichens and mold spores.

Inspired to Write

Seven years after Beatrix wrote about Peter Rabbit to Noel, she was **inspired** to publish the tale as a book. Every publisher she contacted rejected the story. Finally, Beatrix decided to print the book herself. *The Tale of Peter Rabbit* was first printed in 1901. It was well-received, and soon more copies were printed.

In 1881, the Natural History Museum of South Kensington officially opened its doors to the public.

When Beatrix was nearly 30 years of age, she wrote a paper about fungi that included detailed illustrations. Beatrix showed her work to her uncle, Sir Henry Roscoe, who was a well-respected scientist. With his help, Beatrix took her works to the Royal Botanic Gardens, where scientific studies about plants take place. The director and other scientists at the gardens thought Beatrix was too young and uneducated to understand what she was drawing. They rejected her work.

Beatrix continued to write about her theories, and her uncle took the writings to meetings at the Linnaean Society of London, a group that reviews scientific evidence. At this time, women were not allowed to attend these meetings. Beatrix's writings were read to the group, but they felt it needed more work before it could be published.

After her studies on fungi were rejected, Beatrix began to draw pictures of her pets again. She also began to try other types of artwork, such as photography and needlework. However, she enjoyed painting over any other art form.

Beatrix drew pictures of Benjamin Bunny. She said he was nice, but sometimes he would bite her.

By the early 1900s, Beatrix was a successful writer and illustrator. She had found a company to publish her books. Beatrix worked closely with her editor, Norman Warne, one of the three brothers who ran the company. Norman was a dear friend, and the two wrote to each other often.

In 1905, Beatrix received a letter from Norman asking her to marry him. Beatrix was excited about their wedding, but she and Norman never married. He died of an illness soon after their engagement.

During this time, Beatrix had been caring for her aging parents. She had never moved out of her parents' home, but she decided to use the money she made from her books to buy a farm, called Hill Top, in the Lake District. Though she did not live at the farm right away, Beatrix visited often. In 1912, Beatrix accepted a marriage proposal from her **solicitor**, William Heelis. The two were married the following year. The couple lived in Castle Cottage, Sawrey, in the Lake District, and Beatrix spent most of her time farming.

Beatrix set many of her stories at her farm, Hill Top.

Favorite Books

After Bertram was sent to boarding school, Beatrix was lonely. She spent many nights reading William Shakespeare's plays. Shakespeare was a well-known British playwright who wrote 38 plays, including *Romeo and Juliet* and *Macbeth*. By 28 years old, Beatrix had memorized at least six of Shakespeare's plays. Beatrix also read Sir Walter Scott's novels and Maria Edgeworth's writings. Well-known books by Sir Walter Scott include *Rob Roy*, *Waverley*, and *The Lady of the Lake*. Maria Edgeworth is best-known for her children's stories. Beatrix would learn the **psalms** by heart and write **hymns**.

Learning the Craft

B eatrix Potter's parents were very **protective** of their daughter. For this reason, she was homeschooled by a governess named Miss Hammond. Miss Hammond encouraged Beatrix to draw and to write stories. She often took Beatrix to the Natural History Museum to study.

By eight years of age, Beatrix was drawing the plants and animals she saw in books and at the museum. A few years later, her parents hired an art teacher to improve Beatrix's talents. Between 1878 and 1883, Beatrix took private art lessons from Miss Cameron. She taught the young girl how to draw **freehand** and paint using watercolors.

Following her time with Miss Cameron, Beatrix took 12 lessons in oil painting. Beatrix preferred drawing and painting with watercolors and soon stopped oil painting.

Beatrix liked to challenge herself. She studied insects through Bertram's microscope.

When she was 15 years old, Beatrix took courses at the Science and Art Department of the Committee of Council for Education. She learned to draw models and paint flowers among other things. She later received an Art Student's Certificate for her work.

Beatrix Potter did not realize her own talents until she began telling her stories to children. Aside from *The Tale of Peter Rabbit*, Beatrix wrote *The Tailor of Gloucester*, *The Tale of Squirrel Nutkin*, and others in letters to her governess's children. The children enjoyed Beatrix's stories, which made her think about publishing her books.

Inspired to Write

Beatrix wanted to know if children would enjoy reading her stories. She would make small picture books by pasting sketches alongside hand-written words. Later, she would use the book as a guide to write and draw the finished piece.

Some of Beatrix's original illustrations are held at London's Tate Gallery.

Getting Published

At first, it was difficult for Beatrix to get her books published. It was hard for women at this time to be taken seriously as writers and artists. After Beatrix's paper on fungi was rejected, she was unsure if she should continue writing.

As a young woman, Beatrix's uncle, Sir Henry Roscoe, urged her to try to sell her art. Beatrix made six drawings of Benjamin Bouncer for Christmas cards. Her brother, Bertram, brought them to Hildesheimer & Faulkner. They liked what they saw and sent Beatrix a small check. They also asked her to send more drawings.

Later, a family friend, Canon Rawnsley, encouraged Beatrix to have her works published. Canon Rawnsley was a published author who was very interested in Beatrix's drawings. He suggested that Beatrix give her sample of *The Tale of Peter Rabbit* to a publishing company called Frederick Warne & Co. They rejected her book, so Beatrix decided to make her own version.

The Publishing Process

Publishing companies receive hundreds of **manuscripts** from authors each year. Only a few manuscripts become books. Publishers must be sure that a manuscript will sell many copies. As a result, publishers reject most of the manuscripts they receive.

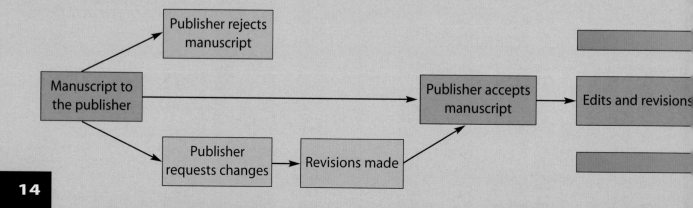

Beatrix approached a printer, and in 1901, 250 copies of her little book were made. Beatrix sold copies of the book to her friends and relatives. She sent a copy of her book to Frederick Warne & Co. They decided to publish a new version of the book. This version would have color pictures instead of black and white. Beatrix set to work redrawing the pictures in color and adding some new ones. When she was done, Frederick Warne & Co. printed 8,000 copies of the new *The Tale of Peter Rabbit*.

Beatrix wrote *The Tailor of Gloucester* one year later. These first two books sold well. In 1903, *The Tale of Squirrel Nutkin* was published, and it was a huge success. Beatrix continued to generate ideas for new books. She went on to publish another 20 books over the next 10 years.

Inspired to Write

One of Beatrix's nursemaids, Miss McKenzie, believed in witches and fairies. Beatrix said that Miss McKenzie's belief in these **mythical** beings helped inspire Beatrix to write.

Once a manuscript has been accepted, it goes through many stages before it is published. Often, authors change their work to follow an editor's suggestions. Once the book is published, some authors receive royalties. This is money based on book sales.

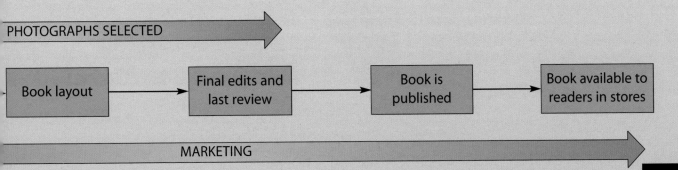

PHOTOGRAPHS SELECTED →

Book layout → Final edits and last review → Book is published → Book available to readers in stores

MARKETING →

Writer Today

Beatrix Potter lived with her parents until she wed in 1913. However, she had bought Hill Top in 1905. When she was not caring for her parents, Beatrix spent a great deal of time farming and sheep herding at the farm. Four years later, she bought more land called Castle Farm.

After Beatrix and William Heelis wed, Beatrix spent little time writing. Instead, she focused on sheep farming. She became an award-winning Herdwick sheep breeder and was elected the first female president of the Herdwick Sheep Breeder's Association.

Beatrix's sheep won many awards at local shows.

During World War I, Beatrix's publisher fell on hard times. To help the company earn more money, Beatrix published another children's book called *Appley Dapply's Nursery Rhymes*, as well as two painting activity books. After this time, Beatrix published only a few more books, including the little book *The Tale of Little Pig Robinson*, which was printed in 1930. The last book published during Beatrix's lifetime was *Sister Anne* in 1932. She did not illustrate the book, and it was only sold in the United States.

By the late 1930s, Beatrix was in poor health. She died in 1943, at Castle Farm in Sawrey. She left most of her property to The National Trust. This is a charity that protects more than 300 historic houses and gardens, as well as many mills, monuments, forests, farms, and castles. Beatrix Potter left Hill Top and about 4,000 acres of land to the Trust.

Beatrix's ashes were spread over the Sawrey countryside.

Popular Books

Beatrix Potter wrote a total of 23 books in her lifetime. Here are some of her most popular tales.

The Tale of Peter Rabbit

The Tale of Peter Rabbit has sold more than 40 million copies around the world. It was the first title in a series of illustrated books. In this book, Peter Rabbit and his three sisters, Mopsy, Flopsy and Cotton-tail live with their mother under a large fir tree. Peter likes to get into mischief. He goes into Mr. McGregor's garden and eats some of Mr. McGregor's vegetables. Mr. McGregor discovers what Peter has done and chases him through the garden. Peter loses his shoes and gets tangled in some netting. He escapes just as Mr. McGregor is about to catch him. Peter runs to the gardening shed and hides in a watering can. Mr. McGregor discovers the hiding place when Peter sneezes. Peter keeps on running from Mr. McGregor and finally makes it home safe. Mr. McGregor makes a scarecrow out of the clothes that Peter Rabbit lost while running away from him. Peter Rabbit does not feel well at dinner, and his mother sends him to bed early with some medicine.

THE TALE OF
PETER RABBIT

BEATRIX POTTER
The original and authorized edition

The Tale of Squirrel Nutkin

The Tale of Squirrel Nutkin is about a little red squirrel who has a large tail. Nutkin goes to gather some nuts on Owl Island with a group of squirrels. Instead of collecting nuts with the others, Nutkin spends all of his time playing. For six days straight, all of the squirrels go to collect nuts on the island, while Nutkin plays or gets into mischief. Every time the squirrels visit the island, they give gifts to Old Brown, the owl that lives there. When Nutkin sees the owl, he dances and sings riddles. Old Brown gets annoyed with Nutkin and captures him. Nutkin escapes, but he loses most of his large, bushy tail.

THE TALE OF
SQUIRREL NUTKIN

BEATRIX POTTER
The original and authorized edition

The Tale of Benjamin Bunny

Benjamin Bunny appears in a few Beatrix Potter books, including *The Tale of the Flopsy Bunnies* and *The Tale of Mr. Tod*. In *The Tale of Benjamin Bunny*, Benjamin and his cousin Peter Rabbit search through Mr. McGregor's garden to try to find the clothes that Peter lost in *The Tale of Peter Rabbit*. This time, Mr. McGregor has gone out with Mrs. McGregor. Benjamin and Peter find the clothes and gather onions from the garden. As they try to leave, Benjamin and Peter spot a cat at the garden gate. The pair are afraid that the cat will hurt them, so they hide under a basket. Benjamin Bunny's father attacks the cat and rescues Benjamin and Peter. They return home, and Peter Rabbit gives his mother the onions. She forgives him for losing his clothes.

The Tailor of Gloucester

The Tailor of Gloucester is about a poor tailor who has a cat and several mice living in his shop. The tailor has many scrap pieces of material that he cannot use, and the mice make themselves clothing from the scraps. The tailor sends his cat, Simpkin, to get him some food and a piece of cherry-colored silk thread. The thread is for a coat that the tailor is making for the mayor's wedding on Christmas morning. While Simpkin is shopping, the tailor lets the mice out from where the cat has trapped them. When Simpkin returns, he finds all of the mice are missing. He gets angry and hides the silk. The tailor becomes ill, so the mice finish making the mayor's coat for him.

The Tale of Tom Kitten

This is a story about three little kittens. Tabitha Twitchit is the mother of these mischievous kittens. One day, Tabitha finds out that guests are coming to visit her. She gathers her children together to wash them and dress them in clean clothes. She tells the kittens that they can play outside if they promise to keep clean. The kittens promptly go outside, get dirty, and lose all of their clothes to some ducks. When the kittens return home, their mother is very angry. She hides them upstairs and tells her guests that the kittens have the measles.

Creative Writing Tips

Beatrix Potter had to practice writing and drawing to perfect her work. She had a great imagination, but she found it difficult to get published. Still, she kept writing and drawing until other people were ready to accept her work. Writers use many techniques to help them tell stories well. Here are some tips that young writers can use to create great stories.

Find Inspiration

Good writers are excited about their subjects. Think about what excites or interests you. It could be a person, an activity, a place, or a dream you have had. Create a list of topics you would enjoy writing about. Describe each topic as if you were telling a story about it. Try to develop a story from these notes.

Peter, Flopsy, Mopsy, and Cotton-tail lived with their mother under a fir tree.

Read

Reading other writers' stories can help you become a better writer. Their stories can help you learn new words, get ideas, and become more knowledgeable about different subjects. Beatrix Potter enjoyed reading books about nature. For her tenth birthday, Beatrix received a book called *Birds Drawn from Nature*, and she became inspired to draw and write about this subject. Visit your local library or educational websites to read about any subject that interests you.

Be Creative

Do not let any boundaries limit your creativity. Beatrix Potter had a broad imagination, and she put her ideas into stories and drawings. Try to illustrate your own story. Develop unusual characters for your stories, such as a talking horse. Being creative will make your stories original. They will stand out from stories written by other writers.

Practice

It takes most writers a long time to perfect their skills. A good way to develop writing skills is to read, take writing classes, and to practice writing. Try writing in a journal every day. This will help you record any ideas that you might have. You can read your journal a year later to see how much your writing has improved.

Inspired to Write

Beatrix Potter was inspired to write by the beauty of the Lake District. She enjoyed the animals and the scenery on the land that she owned in the area.

Beatrix used animals to illustrate nursery rhymes, such as *The Old Woman Who Lived in a Shoe.*

Writing a Biography Review

A biography is an account of an individual's life that is written by another person. Some people's lives are very interesting. In school, you may be asked to write a biography review. The first thing to do when writing a biography review is to decide whom you would like to learn about. Your school library or community library will have a large selection of biographies from which to choose.

Are you interested in an author, a sports figure, an inventor, a movie star, or a president? Finding the right book is your first task. Whether you choose to write your review on a biography of Beatrix Potter or another person, the task will be similar.

Begin your review by writing the title of the book, the author, and the person featured in the book. Then, start writing about the main events in the person's life. Include such things as where the person grew up and what his or her childhood was like. You will want to add details about the person's adult life, such as whether he or she married or had children. Next, write about what you think makes this person special. What kinds of experiences influenced this individual? For instance, did he or she grow up in unusual circumstances? Was the person determined to accomplish a goal? Include any details that surprised you. A concept web is a useful research tool. Use the concept web on the right to begin researching your biography review.

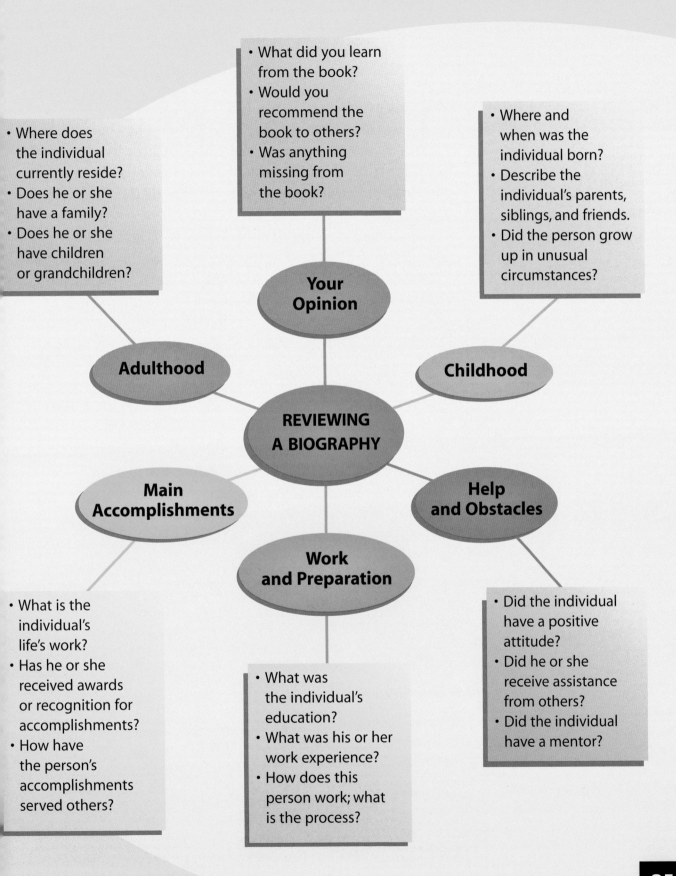

- What did you learn from the book?
- Would you recommend the book to others?
- Was anything missing from the book?

- Where and when was the individual born?
- Describe the individual's parents, siblings, and friends.
- Did the person grow up in unusual circumstances?

- Where does the individual currently reside?
- Does he or she have a family?
- Does he or she have children or grandchildren?

Your Opinion

Adulthood

Childhood

REVIEWING A BIOGRAPHY

Main Accomplishments

Help and Obstacles

Work and Preparation

- What is the individual's life's work?
- Has he or she received awards or recognition for accomplishments?
- How have the person's accomplishments served others?

- What was the individual's education?
- What was his or her work experience?
- How does this person work; what is the process?

- Did the individual have a positive attitude?
- Did he or she receive assistance from others?
- Did the individual have a mentor?

Fan Information

Today, Beatrix Potter fans can remember the writer and artist by visiting Hill Top. Hill Top has been restored to look exactly as it did when Beatrix lived there. The former offices of William Heelis in Hawkshead now house the Beatrix Potter Gallery, where some of Beatrix's letters and drawings are on display.

Beatrix's fans can visit the World of Beatrix Potter Attraction in Bowness in the Lakes, England. Here, visitors can walk through life-like scenes from all 23 tales by Beatrix Potter. The attraction features short films and exhibits about Beatrix's life, and visitors can have tea with Peter Rabbit.

Many of Beatrix Potter's works have been stored with The National Trust or in museums. The National Trust has many first edition copies of her books and more than 700 watercolors and ink drawings. It also has furniture from Hill Top and copies of some of Beatrix's manuscripts and her personal items, including a set of place mats that Beatrix hand painted. The Warne Archive of Beatrix's letters artwork and more is housed at the Victoria & Albert Museum in London, England. The museum also owns many of Beatrix's original letters and artwork.

Together, the Warne Archive and the Victoria and Albert Museum contain the largest collection of Beatrix's original work.

Since Beatrix's death, several movies and plays have been made about her books and her life. In 1971, a film called *The Tales of Beatrix Potter* used ballet dancers and music to tell many of Beatrix's stories. In 1982, *The Tale of Beatrix Potter*, a fact-based movie about the writer's life, was released. Another movie, *Miss Potter*, was released in 2006. It is a romantic movie about Beatrix's life with Norman.

A number of books have been written about Beatrix Potter. Linda Lear wrote *Beatrix Potter: A Life in Nature*. This biography was published in 2006. Fans can learn about Beatrix Potter's life by reading her diary, *The Journal of Beatrix Potter, 1881-1897*, which was published in 1966. The diary includes a great deal of information about Beatrix's family. *Beatrix Potter: Artist, Storyteller & Countrywoman* by Judy Taylor is another great source for information about Beatrix.

Renée Zellweger starred as Beatrix in the movie *Miss Potter*.

WEB LINKS

Beatrix's Official Website
www.peterrabbit.com

Visitors to this site can learn more about Beatrix Potter, her artwork, and her books. They can keep up to date with Beatrix Potter events and news from around the world.

The Beatrix Potter Society
www.beatrixpottersociety.org.uk

This site has information about the Beatrix Potter Society, which was formed in 1980 by people who are dedicated to the upkeep of Beatrix's past works.

Quiz

1

Q: How many tales did Beatrix Potter write?

A: She wrote 23 tales.

2

Q: What did Beatrix study at the Natural History Museum?

A: She studied fungi.

3

Q: Who encouraged Beatrix to have her books published?

A: Canon Rawnsley encouraged Beatrix.

4

Q: How did Beatrix write in her secret diary?

A: She wrote in a secret code that only she could understand.

7

Q: When was Beatrix's last little book published?

A: The last little book was published in 1930.

5

Q: Where are many of Beatrix's original pieces now kept?

A: The National Trust, the Warne Archive, and the Victoria and Albert Museum have many of her works.

8

Q: What was the first book that Beatrix published?

A: *The Tale of Peter Rabbit* **was the first book she published.**

9

Q: What was the name of the first farm Beatrix bought?

A: Beatrix's first farm was Hill Top.

6

Q: What company first published Beatrix's drawings?

A: Hildesheimer & Faulkner published *The Happy Pair.*

10

Q: When did Beatrix die?

A: Beatrix died in 1943.

Writing Terms

This glossary will introduce you to some of the main terms in the field of writing. Understanding these common writing terms will allow you to discuss your ideas about books and writing with others.

action: the moving events of a work of fiction

antagonist: the person in the story who opposes the main character

autobiography: a history of a person's life written by that person

biography: a written account of another person's life

character: a person in a story, poem, or play

climax: the most exciting moment or turning point in a story

episode: a short piece of action, or scene, in a story

fiction: stories about characters and events that are not real

foreshadow: hinting at something that is going to happen later in the book

imagery: a written description of a thing or idea that brings an image to mind

narrator: the speaker of the story who relates the events

nonfiction: writing that deals with real people and events

novel: published writing of considerable length that portrays characters within a story

plot: the order of events in a work of fiction

protagonist: the leading character of a story; often a likable character

resolution: the end of the story, when the conflict is settled

scene: a single episode in a story

setting: the place and time in which a work of fiction occurs

theme: an idea that runs throughout a work of fiction

Glossary

carriages: vehicles that have four wheels and are pulled by horses

commissioned: to be hired by a company or person and paid to do specific work

freehand: to draw without the aid of tools, such as a ruler

fungi: a spongy, abnormal plant-like organism, such as yeast, mold, and mushrooms

governesses: women that are hired to raise and teach a child

hymns: songs of praise

inspired: to be influenced positively by something

Lake District: England's largest national park

manuscripts: original texts of an author's work

mythical: fictional beings that appear in folk tales and legends

protective: very caring and guarding

psalms: a book of the Bible that has 150 songs, hymns, and prayers

solicitor: a lawyer who deals with certain legal matters

theories: ideas used to explain something

Index

Photo Credits

Every reasonable effort has been made to trace ownership and to obtain permission to reprint copyright material. The publishers would be pleased to have any errors or omissions brought to their attention so that they may be corrected in subsequent printings.

Photo Credits: All images reproduced with the permission of Warne & Co. Getty Images: pages 1, 3, 4, 7, 9, 11 bottom, 12, 13, 16 left, 16 right, 17, 20 bottom, 26, 27; newscom: pages 8, 10, 11 top, 22, 23; Warne & Co.: pages 18, 19, 20 top, 21.

Thank you to Frederick Warne & Co. for their help with the manuscript.